BOOK W ORMS

## Our Holidays

# Celebrate Halloween

**Mary-Lou Smith**

Cavendish
Square

New York

Published in 2016 by Cavendish Square Publishing, LLC
243 5th Avenue, Suite 136, New York, NY 10016

Library of Congress Cataloging-in-Publication Data

Smith, Mary-Lou, 1960-
Celebrate Halloween / Mary-Lou Smith.
pages cm. — (Our holidays)
Includes index.
ISBN 978-1-50260-416-3 (hardcover)
ISBN 978-1-50260-415-6 (paperback)
ISBN 978-1-50260-417-0 (ebook)
1. Halloween—Juvenile literature. I. Title.

GT4965.S59 2016
394.2646—dc23

2014049160

Editorial Director: David McNamara
Editor: Kristen Susienka
Copy Editor: Cynthia Roby
Art Director: Jeffrey Talbot
Designer: Joseph Macri
Senior Production Manager: Jennifer Ryder-Talbot
Production Editor: Renni Johnson

Printed in the United States of America

# Contents

Today is Halloween.

Halloween is on October 31.

**4**

# OCTOBER

| Sunday | Monday | Tuesday | Wednesday | Thursday | Friday | Saturday |
|--------|--------|---------|-----------|----------|--------|----------|
|  |  | 1 | 2 | 3 | 4 | 5 |
| 6 | 7 | 8 | 9 | 10 | 11 | 12 |
| 13 | 14 | 15 | 16 | 17 | 18 | 19 |
| 20 | 21 | 22 | 23 | 24 | 25 | 26 |
| 27 | 28 | 29 | 30 | 31 |  |  |

5

There are many **traditions** on Halloween.

One is to go to a pumpkin patch and pick out a pumpkin.

Erica, Dani, and Jeremiah carve pumpkins together.

9

We light our pumpkins and put them on display.

We make **candy apples**, too.

13

We wear **costumes** and eat treats.

14

15

One of the most fun things
to do on Halloween is
trick or treat.

You visit your neighbors and
when the door opens, you say,
"Trick or treat!"

16

17

Our neighbors give us candy.

**18**

Halloween is a fun holiday.

How do you celebrate Halloween?

21

# New Words

**candy apples** (KAN-dee AP-pulhs)  Apples dipped in caramel or chocolate and decorated with candy sprinkles.

**costumes** (KOS-toomz)  Outfits worn to make you look like someone else.

**traditions** (tra-DIH-shunz)  Events you do every year during holidays, such as trick or treating.

**22**

# Index

**23**

# About the Author

**Mary-Lou Smith** likes to write books, crochet, and bake desserts. She lives in Boston, Massachusetts, with her dog, Bagpipes.

## About

Bookworms help independent readers gain reading confidence through high-frequency words, simple sentences, and strong picture/text support. Each book explores a concept that helps children relate what they read to the world in which they live.